Making Sense of My Feelings as a Teen Going Through Puberty with Autism

Travis E. Breeding

Copyright © 2012 Travis E. Breeding

All rights reserved.

ISBN: 978-1480135607
ISBN-13: 978-1480135604

DEDICATION

This book is dedicated to Teens throughout the world who are on the Autism spectrum. Being a teenager is a challenging time. Throwing Autism and Puberty in the mix only makes it more confusing and trying. It is my hope, by sharing experiences in this book that you'll understand more of what it's like to live as a teen with Autism dealing with this on a daily basis.

CONTENTS

1	Asperger's Syndrome	6
2	Aspie Mind "Reality of Living within Two Worlds	11
3	Sex	19
4	Sex and TV	24
5	I'm A Late Bloomer	26
6	The Special Interests Role	33
7	Appendix	44
	About the Author	60
	Autism Books and Resources	61

1 ASPERGER'S SYNDROME

October 30th 2007: A day that would change my life. This was a day that I received the answer to the question I had been seeking for 5 to 10 years. What was wrong with me?

I had spent the last year seeing psychologist seeking out answers. None seemed to be able to provide me with a reason to why I was struggling with social interaction and making friends. However, on that day, "Congratulations," the doctor said, you have Asperger's Syndrome.

Up until this point, my life did not make any sense to me. I had always struggled with making friends and could not maintain a friendship to save my life. I tried to explain myself to several psychologists who looked at me as if I was puzzling to them. I knew there was something going on with me but had no idea what it was. I felt as if I was on the outside looking in. It is like looking through a window and being able to see what is going on outside but being locked inside and unable to get out. Now I know why I was puzzling.

Asperger's Syndrome is probably the most complex thing I have ever studied. This makes me the most complex thing I have ever studied as well. Asperger's Syndrome is often referred to as the 'invisible disability' says Dr. Tony Attwood, author of <u>The Complete Guide to Asperger's Syndrome.</u>

Asperger's is not something that affects me physically. Sure, I may have some balance issues from time to time but you can argue that any neurotypical can struggle with basic coordination skills from time to time. I do not appear to be any different from the next guy. Looking at me from the outside, no one would ever know that I have Autism. It is invisible and therefore it complicates things in some ways but makes some things easier as well.

Asperger's Syndrome will affect each one of us in different ways. To me, it is one of the most interesting things in the world because it involves such a wide spectrum of things and a huge variety of symptoms. It ranges from a non-verbal child desperately trying to communicate his wants and needs to a high functioning person who can function on their own but is just socially awkward or quirky. I find that many people are unaware of how often they rely on basic social skills to get them through a situation or to finish their day.

Most individuals with AS are very intelligent. We thrive when allowed to work within our areas of special interest. Adaptive skills on the other hand, are skills that we all need to have mastered in order to care for ourselves. People with Asperger's Syndrome can struggle with these seemingly basic life skills. A seemingly simple task, such as taking a shower, can be hard for someone with AS. People with Asperger's Syndrome also have many strengths in life. They can and do make wonderful friends and employees if given the right support.

There are a number of other challenges associated with Asperger's Syndrome. Rather than spend time here reiterating what those are, we would instead to refer you to Dr. Tony Attwood's books and his website, listed in our resources section.

My Asperger's Syndrome diagnosis came in October of 2007, when I was 22. Like so many others, I received a late diagnosis in life. I was behind the game and needed fast intervention if I was going to catch up to my peers. Because people with AS are so high functioning many do not even see them as having a disability. This is a good thing in many instances, but sometimes it can create some serious problems.

One major problem it can cause is unemployment. As many as 80-90% of people with AS are unemployed. There are many of us sitting around with great, useful skills we can provide an employer, but because we have problems understanding the social scene we cannot seem to find fitting employment. We struggle with interviewing and when hired we need to have certain supports lined up to ensure a successful transition. There are a number of great books out there on Asperger's Syndrome and employment; we have included some in the resource section of this book.

Another problem with Asperger's being an 'invisible disability' is that many people believe individuals with disability do not have any interest in having sex. I hear this myth all the time and we will spend the majority of this text telling you it simply is not true.

Having autism does not define me. Nor does it change who I am. It does not present any inherent limitations either. It just presents some challenges that others do not have to face. However, everyone has his or her own challenges in life and therefore we have a lot more in common then you think.

Some of us cannot walk. Some cannot talk. Nevertheless, we are all human beings and deserve to be loved and respected.

I often get tired of being treated like a "thing or object" by my peers. I grew up on the outside looking in and felt frustrated that I could not develop the friendships as others were. It seemed as if I was trying to fight my way through a brick wall. I am writing this book and sharing my very own personal stories to show that there are people with "disabilities" if that is what you want to call us, that have the same wants and needs as people without "disabilities." I do not like to use the word "disability" so I use the word "challenges" instead.

I got information from so many terrible resources throughout my journey. I will share what some of those were with you so you can help your child avoid the same trap.

Before receiving my diagnosis of Asperger's Syndrome, I was just a lost boy who could not fit in. When I received my diagnosis, I became the label for a couple of years. I fell into the trap of letting my diagnosis define me for a long time. This made my life more difficult and had to change. I sought help from any resource I could find. I was looking for a sense of belonging.

2 THE ASPIE MIND "REALITY OF LIVING WITHIN TWO WORLDS

I am sure we have all looked at someone and wondered just what they are doing. They seem so out of it and lost. If you have a child with autism, you probably encounter this quite often. I hear so many parents say "if I could just experience their world for one day." While it isn't possible yet to get inside of someone else's brain and know exactly what thoughts and feelings they are having without communicating with them, I will attempt to share some of what I was feeling and do feel when I find myself in a period of isolation and loneliness. I will explain how my make believe/imaginary world works and talk about why this is beneficial for someone on the autism spectrum.

It is important to remember to keep in mind when we reading this, Dr. Stephen Shore's statement, "If you've met one person with autism, you've really only met one person with autism." It is also true that, if you have heard one person with autism describe what their make believe world is like and how they process their thoughts and feelings, then you've only really heard how one person processes those thoughts and feelings.

If I am watching a movie and mom calls me, "Travis, Travis, come do your laundry". I do not seem to hear her or realize that she is talking to me. I am watching one of my favorite movies on television and I seem to not notice she is there. I am lost in the movie and do not know that the real world exists. Why is this? Is this normal?

We are all aware of what "daydreaming" is and how we can get lost in the moment. Some of us get more lost than others do. I have found some people daydream for a moment or two but then they come back to reality and are able to comprehend what is going on in the real world. For me daydreaming is more than just a dream. It is a way of life. It is a coping mechanism for me with Asperger's Syndrome. I daydream as an escape when things are not working as I would like them to socially; when I am feeling socially isolated and rejected. When I am lonely, this daydreaming state is a coping mechanism that allows me to escape the realness of the real world and go into my own make-believe world where I can control my situations and outcomes. It is a safe haven for me.

Dr. Tony Attwood talks about people with Asperger's Syndrome creating a make believe world inside their heads. He often states this can also be a result of "escaping into imagination." I have done this a lot in my life. As a child, I can remember doing this while I was in school. At recess on the playground, I saw the other students running around with each other having a great time and so wanted to be like them but for some reason I was not. It led to me feeling sad and depressed even as a child.

I was not aware of what I was doing at the time, but as an adult, I now know that I was imagining my own world. I was trying to escape the real world or real situation and create my own. I am very good at this and so are many people with autism. Not only is it a coping mechanism for me, but also it was also like having make-believe friends. I remember pretending to be a superhero while on the playground and flying around saving everyone. I used to have so much fun just by being in my make believe world. Not only was it enjoyable there, but also it was also very safe and comforting. I was controlling how my world was going and there were not any outside factors causing me any harm or confusion.

Teachers sometimes had to yell my name just to get my attention, but they certainly were not yelling at me for the same reasons they yelled at other kids. Many kids liked to cause trouble; I never understood the point of intentionally causing trouble or harm to someone. However, many kids throughout my school years that did this. It is stunning to me that this seemed to get worse as we got older and entered middle school. I think a lot of times the fact that I found comfort in watching a movie also lead to my ability to create a make believe world and escape into my imagination.

I often sat at home because there was nothing else to do. In middle school, I watched television or rented movies from the local video store. I remember that this used to be what I would look forward to on the weekends. I would just sit at home and watch movies. The characters in the movies became my friends; they were the ones who were always there for me. For instance, there was a Cameron Diaz movie called, "Head Above Water." Cameron Diaz, or her character Natalie, became my best friend from the movie - she was someone who would always be there, all I had to do was push play on the VCR or DVD player and there she was. She was talking and interacting. In my mind, I would have conversations with her. I processed thoughts and talked to her about things that were going on in my life, but then also things dealing with the movie. It was as if she was my best friend; someone to whom I could relate and not judgmental.

The ability to create this pretend situation/make believe world is something that many people that are not living with autism do not fully understand. It is hard to imagine something that you cannot experience. While it is great to have this ability to escape into imagination and create the make-believe world, it can also become a challenge. The challenges becomes trying to balance that make believe world with the real world that we really live in. "The reality of living within two worlds."

For me it all started when I was in the second grade. There was a group of kids playing on the playground by the swing set. I went up to them and started trying to join their game. They did not like this very much at all. They ended up laughing at me and running away and taking their game somewhere else. I felt so rejected. "Why did they do that?" I asked myself. It did not seem very nice. I slowly lowered my head and walked back to stand next to the teacher on the playground desperately wanting recess to be over for the day. This scene repeated itself daily. My same attempt at social interaction met with the same rejection by my peers. Today, I know that making the same attempt at social interaction in the exact same way each and everyday is obviously going to get the same result each day. However, as we know the Asperger's mind is very black and white. All I knew was the same way to approach my classmates.

To me, there are two steps. There is step 1 and step 10. I often skip straight from step 1 to step 10. I am not able to see the steps in-between. Steps 2-9 are non-existent for me. I know that steps 2-9 are there I am just not able to see what they are. I can even read about them in technical terms or get an idea. Nevertheless, I am not able to visualize them in my mind. I am a visual thinker so I need to be able to visualize a situation or a step in my head before I can take it.

This brings up an interesting point. We often hear of people on the spectrum who might see a social situation unfolding in a movie and then they go out in public in the real world and try to recreate that situation. Why is this? I am able to process those social situations in my head, of which I have a direct visualization. If I am able to see a social situation from the outside, I quickly take mental notes of the situation and what happened. I will then proceed to keep those notes in my mind, go out, and try to use those notes in a social interaction attempt. The problem with this is that on television there are time constraints and other contributing factors that make that social situation skewed and inaccurate. Television is not a good social-skills teaching too for people with Asperger's.

You might ask, why not observe social situations in person and apply what I see to my daily social interactions? The problem with this is that when I am there in the moment, I am so intently focused on what I already know and am trying to process those thoughts, to later use and practice, that I'm not able to effectively observe the socialization overtures others are making. Even when I am in a group with a few people, I am unable to observe their reactions and how they are processing the social situation. This is because I so intently focus on trying to say the right thing or do the right thing, or even make the right body language gesture that I tire and cannot process anything else from the social situation.

Therefore, in a way, I am better able to observe social situations in movies, take that knowledge, and apply it to my life. This is because for a movie I am just sitting there observing and watching. I am not trying to process what is going on in the real world. I am able to focus on the movie and what is going on during the movie. I can also re-watch the scene and look for more social cues. I cannot do that when I am with a group of people. Unfortunately, this means that some of my social actions continue to be skewed.

I have read a bit about an approach to social skills development that involves teaching people on the autism spectrum social skills through the production of a musical. The writers create the musical in the manner in which special real life social situations would occur; in a way that each character in the musical would be practicing real life social situations. However, because there is a script for the musical the actors would not have to work as hard at taking in all of the nonverbal cues along with processing the social thinking: they just follow the script and act in their roles.

I think this is a method from which we will benefit in the future. There is definitely more research to be done here and I am interested in seeing where this will lead. However, you can quickly see the comparison with a movie and a musical. The difference would be that the musical design features real life social situations that may present themselves in our day-to-day lives, not scenes skewed or overdone by Hollywood. This just might be an easy, visual way for us to learn social skills. It is role playing, but playing a real role in a real life situation.

3 SEX

Sex is not a dirty word. Sex is something people talk about all the time. We have to lose the stereotype that people with disabilities are uninterested in it. Ignorance is not bliss. We cannot take a chance with what might happen when a child develops an interest in this area, but has not been properly educated. I think in general, with ABA, we are doing a great job of providing education for children on the autism spectrum. We are even doing a better job of providing information and resources for adults. However, for teenagers and adults with Asperger's, puberty and sexual development can be a very confusing time.

I maintain that Asperger's does not make me less interested in, or attracted to girls or have less of an interest in intimacy. It simply makes it harder for me to understand the appropriate ways for going about meeting my needs in this area. I have spent many years trying to figure it all out, and still struggle to find myself in the company of a woman with whom there is mutual interest.

I want to make sure that other kids don't grow up trying to change who they are like I did for many years and facing the same struggles. I think this book can be a big part of that for teens of today and tomorrow. I wasted a lot of time trying to change who I was as a person, due to my not being properly educated about dating, relationships, and sexuality. I engaged in a lot of inappropriate behavior as a young adult in my early twenties; I got a lot of bad dating and 'pick-up' advice from guys I thought were my friends, but who were really getting a laugh at my expense.

My biggest problem was showing intense interest in the opposite sex. I had a special interest in women. I wanted to date so desperately like my peers but could not figure it out. Because I did not know how to approach these types of situations and had obsessive thoughts and behaviors, I was ridiculed and made fun of by my peers and was also misunderstood by many people. People called me many names as a young adult. Creepy, psycho, weirdo, you name it.

That name-calling has had a lasting effect on me. It is only recently that I have been able to move on from that and let it go; it is now part of my past. It was a learning experience. I have learned much about dating, relationships, and sexuality in the past 3 to 5 years. The problem for me was that it was 10 years too late. The goal is to not allow sexuality education to come 10 years too late for your child or client.

I will share with you a story about a girl I really liked. I met her at college. I met her for the first time on Facebook and we chatted. I was telling her how I thought girls hated me and I did not fit in with anyone. I told her how I had no friends and was so confused about my life. This happened about 6 months before I received my diagnosis.

The first time we hung out, we went to a hockey game. We had a great time and we shared many laughs. I enjoyed my time with her. I started sending her flowers right away. This is where I was making some big mistakes. At first, the flower thing was not too bad but then I started finding her car on campus and leaving them on her vehicle. We hung out about three more times after that. I liked her a lot and it was the first time in my life I ever really spent time one on one with a girl. I did other things that violated the social rules, like calling her school's volleyball coach to see if she could try out.

Unfortunately, however, I was missing so many social boundaries and nuances needed to maintain the friendship and relationship. I just liked her and wanted to make her happy. I would have done anything to see her smile. I failed to realize the inappropriateness of my actions.

I was presenting several of the classic characteristics related to Asperger's Syndrome throughout my entire friendship with this girl and I did not even know I had AS. I was showing an intense interest in one person who I really did not know that well. I was coming on too strong and ignoring unwritten social boundaries. I also took things that she said out of context and thought they meant something they did not.

Later I learned the mistakes I was making because I was unaware of social boundaries or unwritten rules. This was by far the hardest time in my life. I was so interested in the girl that I could not let it go. I ended up calling and texting her pleading with her to like me and just give me a chance. The more I tried the further she ran. It ended up that she was so scared and thought I was going to stalk her. She had to get away from my obsessive behavior and interest in her.

This was a tough spot in which to be. I really felt like I was just being nice. I thought I was doing good things. I was just being me. Being who you are is a great thing, but being who you are without proper social skills and education can cause others around you to be uncomfortable.

That whole situation caused me to have problems with depression and I had a major depressive episode over it. I thought I was the problem; I blamed myself. Kids need to know that if they are experiencing a lot of social rejection or encountering situations, as I was that it is not their fault; it is not because of who they are. It is because of skills they do not have and rules of which they are unaware. It is because of being uneducated on important subjects like dating, relationships, and sexuality. This is why it is so important for us to tackle these issues. We cannot be afraid or embarrassed to discuss or teach them. We must embrace the challenge and help everyone on the autism spectrum live a better life.

4 SEX AND TV

I once read a story about an 18 year old with Asperger's Syndrome who took a line he heard an actor use on an actress in a movie. The line was "I want to have sex with you." He took this line and used it on a classmate of his. Obviously there were some problems involved with using this in a real situation with a girl. What this young gentleman with Asperger's syndrome was missing was the context of the relationship that the two had developed in the movie was not the same as the context of the relationship between him and his classmate.

People with Asperger's syndrome can be very black and white. This means we either fully understand something or we have great difficulty in understanding things. When the young man heard the line "I want to have sex with you" in the movie, he immediately thought that he could take this line and apply it to his every day life. The though process is, "He said it and it worked so if I say the same line it should work too.

It is important for parents to keep an eye on the child and make sure he or she clearly understands that scenes they see from movies are not always accurate. Things are taken out of context and warped. There is also have the time component. For example, in a movie, a guy may meet a girl and be married to her by the end of the movie. People with Asperger's syndrome often miss this time component and it is important to help them comprehend this.

5 I'M A LATE BLOOMER

Individuals on the autism spectrum hit developmental milestones at a later age than their peers do. This was definitely true for me. We are not just talking about the physical developmental milestones such as learning how to talk and walk, although those are some of our best early indicators that there may be something going on with regards to autism.

I also experienced quite a bit of social and emotional developmental delays. I look back at my life now and realize that I developed interests in things that a boy would typically be interested in at a much older age than my peers did. Individuals with Asperger's are about 33 % behind their physical age in regards to social skills. This means that you may have a 12-year-old child with the social and emotional capacity of an 8-year-old.

This is quite an interesting concept because when children are younger there is less of a gap. As your child and his peers age, the gap begins to grow and they become further apart in social and emotional capacity. For me this gap did not really begin to grow until the fifth grade.

Right before I was to switch schools and begin going to middle school, which would be the biggest change of my life, I started to fall behind my peers in the areas of social and emotional capacity. I was not as advanced as they were with social skills but I also was not as far along with being able to feel empathy for someone.

I know there were times when I was sitting with peers wanting to talk about something that might have been my special interest when they would ignore me or laugh at me and push me away. Often times I was told I was annoying. This did not help to make me feel good about myself.

In first grade, the 33 % gap is not a huge deal. A 6-year-old with the social and emotional capacity of a 4 year old is not too far apart. By the time fifth grade comes along, we are looking at a wider gap in number of years. This puts the other students way ahead of some of our kids on the spectrum.

This is a perfect example of why early intervention is important. As we reach the upper grades of Elementary School (3rd, 4th, and 5th grades), this gap begins to grow. Applied Behavior Analysis is a great tool for trying to help bridge this gap. ABA is great for intervening and teaching adaptive and social skills. From my experience, I know that the behaviors and skills I had weren't going to change until I was able to get some help changing them. This holds true today as an adult too. My behaviors do not just change themselves. I have to provide myself with some reinforcement.

A personal example of this delayed development of age appropriate interests is in the area of dating. I went all through middle school and high school without having a real interest in the opposite sex. The other guys were developing this interest by the time middle school had arrived if not before. I was too interested in playing my trombone or doing things that I wanted to do. I was involved in my special interest and the social stuff did not mean much to me at that point.

Things suddenly changed as I hit the age of 19 or 20. I was very late in developing an interest in dating and relationships, but nonetheless the interest came and it came with full force. The problem that arose was because I was not interested in it before and I was often excluded from my peers, so I did not know much about dating or women. It was like jumping in to the pool without knowing the temperature of the water. It was very scary for me.

It is important that parents are not fooled by a child's lack of interest in dating and relationships or sexuality. It is going to come along at some point and time. The question is not if but when. I have encountered a few parents who tell me their child has no interest in dating. I want to caution parents that this is just a developmental delay and in most cases will not be a permanent delay.

Therefore: Talk to your children. If the only education they are getting on puberty and sexuality is from the section of a class they had in 5th grade then we will have many problems when the kids get older. If they are not asking questions, get involved. Ask them what they know about sex. At a young age, some of them will give you the "ew gross" response and that is fine but make sure you are keeping up with what they are interested in knowing about.

Your child will likely start asking questions about puberty. Puberty is a tough time for people on the autism spectrum. Again, this is something that many kids talk about in peer groups as they start to compare what is going on with themselves to others. Being on the spectrum, I never had good peer friendships at that age and did not have anyone to talk with about it. The only people with whom I would have been able to talk about it were my parents, and we did not ever have a conversation like that. I now know how beneficial it would have been to have just had some education on what was going on with my body.

I thought there was something seriously wrong with myself. You might find that your kids have questions about what is going on with their bodies. Some boys might want to know why their growing hair under their arms and girls are definitely going to be asking questions about the menstrual cycle especially if you they were not provided with any education about this. We know how one little thing can cause one of our kids to have a huge meltdown. Well the last thing you want is for a girl to begin her period while she is at school not knowing what is going on. Chances of a meltdown will increase significantly.

I was made fun of because I was not in tune with today's terms in the sexuality world. As I entered High School, it became very age appropriate for guys to start talking about girls and I would imagine the girls to start talking about guys as well. The guys would make comments about the girl and I would sometimes catch on but did not always follow the conversation. It is important that your kids get used to hearing the language in sexuality from a young age. When explaining sexuality we have to use real language like penis and vagina. They need to have full comprehension on what these words mean for several reasons. The most important reason would be for them to protect themselves from sexual predators who might be taking advantage of them. They also need to hear and be familiar with the slang that their peers are likely to use in the locker room.

When I was going through my states of depression, many times I would feel like an alien. I felt this way because of the way others treated me in social situations and in the real world. Yes, I really used to think, on a weekly and even daily basis, that maybe I really was on this planet by mistake and belonged on a different planet. Oddly enough, there is a social networking site, which is a great place for anyone on the autism spectrum to connect with others on the spectrum called "Wrongplanet.net" which was founded by Alex Plank. The site is an amazing place to share personal stories and experiences in dealing with autism spectrum disorders. The reality of it is that with all of the social rejection and isolation one with Asperger's syndrome may experience in life it is easy to quickly think that you were put here in the wrong place or planet and belong some where else. This thought may indeed be a distorted thought but to someone living through this the thought can be very real and discouraging.

Just like with special interests those of us with autism often have, we need to make sure the special interest is moderated and controlled for the safety of the child, likewise, we have to make sure that escaping into imagination and creating a make believe world as a coping mechanism doesn't become harmful to the individual. I think many of the coping mechanisms that I use can be very helpful but can also be hurtful to the development of my self-esteem.

6 THE SPECIAL INTERESTS ROLE

Parents can't say the words "I love you" to their child enough. These are very powerful words but yet it's more than just saying the words. Just as you know saying I love you to your wife or girlfriend involves much more than saying the word. It's the actions that really make a difference.

If your child likes hugs, give them hugs. If they liked to be squeezed find something that can be used to squeeze them. Dr. Temple Grandin is known for inventing her squeeze machine. This was a machine that she used to feel pressure and calm her down when she was in sensory overload.

There's a classic example of this in the movie "Adam" where a woman is wanting to buy a telescope. She's at a party and just having small talk with this gentleman named Adam and he starts giving here the facts about telescopes. These aren't facts that most people would know. In fact you might say he was reciting a scientific paper that would tell you everything you would ever need to know about telescopes. He was way over her head and instead of appreciating his intelligence she thought his social awkwardness was weird. This is a common misunderstanding I find in life and something I think we need to work as a whole.

Middle school is the area where we typically start to see the gap growing between neurotypicals and children with Asperger's Syndrome. This is the time when kids broaden their social skills capacity and start to have small talk and gossip. This becomes highly social and relies on a lot of non-verbal communication and facial expressions.

A Make Believe World

From an early age children with autism escape into imagination and create a make believe world. I've decided that for me it was a way of coping and dealing with the reality of social rejection. I couldn't find acceptance in real life so I created my own make believe world as a defense mechanism in order to cope.

In my make believe world I have control over what's going on. I could like anyone I want. Play with anything I wanted at anytime and pretty much control my environment. It was great to be able to go into that world and escape the troubles of the real world. There was a lot of pain from rejection in the real world and if I could just get away for a few minutes or hours at a time I could feel some relief.

The problem with being in the make believe world is that you can never ever actually live a life in the world that you've created. I know of instances where some parents who have teenagers on the autism spectrum will shelter them from the real world. I've seen parents not allow their kids to go to a peer get together or a friends birthday party because they were afraid their child would be ridiculed or made fun of.

I definitely understand the parent's concern on this issue. I've been the kid getting ridiculed and made fun of on several occasions. It's not fun. But as an adult I'm looking back wishing my parents could have sent me to more of those functions and gatherings. It's not how we fall that matters it is how we get back up that's the most important. We can't learn to do something in life unless we're willing to try. I encourage parents to cautiously let their friends go to a party at peers house where you know the other parents. Just keep an eye from the outside as to what's going on, how your child's being treated, and then come up with a game plan to help teach him some skills he's lacking. I can assure you that just being in an environment like that with other kids his age is going to boost his confidence and he'll probably even learn a few skills on his own. This is a great opportunity for children on the spectrum to grow and I fringe when I hear parents say they can't let their child go to anyone else's house.

It Happened

Nature will be nature. There's nothing you can do as parents that's going to prevent it from happening. Your children will have their first errection and experience with mastribating. There's just no way of preventing it.

For me this occurred at the age of 16. I'd just returned from a choir trip to New York City in the middle of May. It was a Saturday afternoon and I was watching a movie in my bedroom. I was alone and really became intently interested in the movie. I can't even explain to you how this happened in a step by step process because it just started. I remember being very scared when white stuff started pouring out of my penis.

I didn't know what this was I just knew it wasn't urine. I thought there was something wrong with me and I was leaking very important fluids that my body needed. I was worried I was going to die. I had no idea that this was a normal act of nature for human beings. I wasn't educated about any of this and that caused me a lot of anxiety and depression. I mean, who do you ask about something like this. I didn't want to walk up to mom and dad and say "Mom, I'm leaking fluid out of my penis and I don't know what it is. Is something wrong with me?" It wasn't a question you would really want to ask your doctor at that stage either. I definitely didn't want to ask my peers at school. I had already been a little scared of going to school because of all the ridicule and rejection I faced each day. But this was something that was private for me. I didn't want to ask them about it and I'm glad I didn't. Had I, I would have been the biggest joke in the school that year and for the rest of my high school career.

So it happened. I had my first errection at the age of 16 and I was unprepared. It's important to make sure teenagers are prepared for this to happen. This doesn't happen for everyone at exactly the same age. In fact for me the age of 16 is a couple years later than most people experience this.

I wish I had known about it before it happened. People with autism and asperger's syndrome typically have a hard time with change. This was quite a big change for me. It's something that I needed to be prepared for. I wish I'd known what to expect. I wish I could have been educated so this wouldn't have been such a tragic event for me. I was mortified.

Because I was unaware of what was going on I did some research online. We must prevent our kids from accessing information online without monitoring them. There are so many things post online that our inappropriate and can lead to more confusion about this stuff. It is very imperative that children are not only educated about these issues but equally as important that you show them a proper way to access information if they aren't comfortable talking to you about it.

Everything I found online made me feel guilty that I was experiencing this. I was made to feel ashamed of myself. I accessed some blogs online where people were talking about Mastribation and some of the comments left on there made me feel like a horrible person. It's simply not true though. Now that I've grown up and accessed proper information from professionals and other valid resources I know that this is a normal thing for a boy to engage in as a teenager and young adult. I carried that guilt around with me for 3 or 4 years because I wasn't sure if it was okay or not. I never talked to anyone about it. Carrying the guilt made my anxiety increase to uncontrollable levels. It is frustrating to me that I had to go all of those years without being able to understand what I was experiencing was perfectly normal.

Late bloomer doesn't mean no bloomer at all. Children with autism are going to grow up and experience the same acts of nature that others are going to as well. It's extra important that kids on the spectrum are prepared for these changes. They have to be prepared for puberty. They need to be taught sexuality so they can stay safe. They need to be taught it so that they don't walk around feeling guilty or thinking there's something wrong with them for years. I know what I could have benefited from as a kid growing up now so I advocate for so many other kids who are younger than me but going to be going through the same thing. Please don't put off discussing the issue of sexuality with your child. They have a right to know and be protected. We must always remember a saying that I will refer to often throughout this book and reference during presentations. "If you don't teach it, someone else will." If you don't educate your child on these issues then they are going to access the information from another source. That could be another person. Or it could be from the internet. The other person might be your child's friends at school.

It's very important that children learn from their parents and not from peers in their classroom.

Below is a journal entry about some feelings I have experienced as an adult with sexuality. The journal entry was entitled "Desire."

The Hidden Desires of an Aspie

By Travis Breeding

You and I are more alike than you think. I like girls just as you. Why do girls hate me but love you? I have wants, needs, and desires just as you. The difference is you are able to communicate this in a proper manner and I am not?

I wonder why girls laugh at me, make fun of me, and call me creepy and weird. I have Asperger's Syndrome and know that I will never have a girlfriend. All I want to experience is an intimate encounter. I want a girlfriend, but getting a kiss would make me melt. Why do girls hate me?

The word creepy may just be a thing that women call guys but to me the word creepy is a horrifying word that I've heard my entire life. No one wants to be creepy and I don't try to be creepy on purpose but I don't understand the hidden curriculum and am socially awkward.

As a 24 year old male with Asperger's Syndrome I have the desire to be intimate. The desire for physical touches, the desire for sexual intercourse but because I have Asperger's Syndrome it is likely this will never happens. People with disabilities want and need sex just as those who don't and I wish others would understand this. I want a girlfriend. This is a huge deal and no one seems to understand.

I have witness girls kiss other guys with ease like there's nothing to it but when I am interested in them they go "ewe gross" you are fat and ugly because you have Asperger's Syndrome. I know a girl who let's gay guys feel her breasts whenever they want to but she would never let me feel hers because I'm an aspie and am weird.

I want to be normal. I want to feel loved and cared for. I want girls to like me but know this will never happen. I feel I have a lot to offer a woman if they'd *just give me a chance but because I have Asperger's I'll likely never get the chance.*

I constantly watch girls get hurt over and over by men who don't even care about them but yet these women are completely into these guys and date them more than the guys who truly care about them. To be honest, Asperger's Syndrome in itself isn't such a bad thing. I can honestly sit here and tell you if it wasn't for the fact that Asperger has caused girls to hate me I wouldn't care if I had it at all. But the fact that it makes girls hate me makes life emotionally painful.

Look at this above journal entry that was written by me three years ago. Because I had no idea what was going on in my life in regards to sexuality and dating I was mortified. I thought there was something severely wrong with me. I carried that feeling around with me for 4 to 5 years. I began to lose control of my feelings and everything else in my life was shutting down. I had completely given up on life at one point due to this. I share this with you so that you can understand just how tragic it can be for someone on the spectrum to not have access to proper education.

I started to receive some help at the age of 25 and really began to access education and help in the past 6 months to a year. I will tell you that learning about sexuality and becoming more comfortable with myself has helped improve my quality of life. Yes I learned late and I'm getting to the goal later in life than others but the important thing is that I'm getting there. My hope is that you'll be able to help your child or client get there sooner than I did.

APPENDIX

In the following section, you'll find an appendix of terms and explanations of things dealing with Asperger's Syndrome. These are topics that were introduced throughout the book and all are related to Autism. I wanted to expand upon some things at the end of the book. This is a great source for a greater explanation of Asperger's Syndrome.

The Reason behind the Special Interest

There are a couple of reasons as to why the special interest develops to such an intense level in an individual on the autism spectrum. I should note that this is only my opinion and you should always consult a professional, but I do believe that getting advice from someone who's experienced this can be very insightful.

Reason Number One

The child on the spectrum doesn't have a normal level of social skills that is up to par with their peers.

I formed a special interest in things because I didn't have the capability to carry on a conversation about things that other kids might have wanted to talk about. This caused me to be excluded from any group of students who was ever congregating or sitting around, talking. When one is excluded from a group, what's left for him to do?

Throughout middle and high school, I would often sit at home and just think about music, practice my trombone nonstop, and listen to jazz recordings to the point to where it became an obsession but also a way to not feel so lonely.

For me, music- and in particular the trombone- was my best friend. I had pretty much lost my best friend. To me, music was my best friend. It was what I liked and it was easy to interact with. There were no social norms or rules to follow to be friends with the music.

The special interest is also something that doesn't go away. People come and go, but things are usually always here and consistent. For a person with Autism or Asperger's Syndrome, losing a friend who's a person can be devastating-not only because we become attached to the person but also because of our lack of ability to make friends. So when we lose a friend, we have to try to make new friends, and this is very stressful for us. I cannot speak for all people with an autism diagnosis, but I can tell you that I'm one who ants friends. I've always wanted to be included in the group. I know that there are some people on the spectrum who don't have an interest in having friendships at all or interacting with others. Then there are some who do but can't talk or communicate in any way at all, which would be extremely frustrating.

To sum things up, the special interest forms because the person with autism is excluded from basically all forms of social interaction by their peers. Without having any social interaction at all, they have a lot of time on their hands, and they spend that time doing something they like. It's just that they spend more time with the thing they are interested in rather than being around other people, which causes the interest to become a friend. In my opinion, the special interest is something that someone on the spectrum uses to cope with not being able to build successful relationships with other people. Because they can't have a friend, they replace the friend with the special interest.

Reason Number 2

Communicating with the special interest is easy and much less stressful than communicating with an NT.

A lot of people just don't realize how stressful and tiring talking to people can be for individuals on the spectrum. It's extremely hard to talk to someone. Just trying to look them in the eye and say hi is a challenge for most of us. Therefore, it is stressful. It's also so much work that it can become tiring. People with autism often report being tired after even just a brief social exchange with someone. This is happening because of the dysfunction in their central nervous system.

It is my opinion that because communication with people is very stressful, challenging, tiring, and yes, frustrating for us on the spectrum that people with autism form a special interest. Think about it. It's so much easier for us to communicate with an object than it is to communicate with a human being. For me, playing trombone comes naturally. I can communicate very well and articulate what I'm saying with it. But when I'm talking to people, I have a hard time communicating. I get misunderstood, and my actions get misinterpreted. I get ridiculed, made fun of, and bullied due to my lack of social understanding and awareness.

When I'm playing my trombone, I can't talk, and I'm not communicating to a person directly. I am communicating to them indirectly by providing a musical sound that they can enjoy. Without having to worry if I'm doing something wrong or unacceptable, I'm able to relax and find much more enjoyment. Even if I was to go bowling in a group or putt-putt golfing, I wouldn't be able to enjoy myself because there is a lot of social interaction expected. So therefore, it's so easy to see why an individual with autism might develop a special interest. Special interests are easy to communicate with, making them virtually stress free. They relieve stress. The individual with autism doesn't have to say anything to them. They don't have to worry about the interest making fun of them or judging them, and they can keep and maintain the relationship at ease for a lifetime.

How do we handle the special interest in an individual with Autism?

I hear a lot of talk from professionals who are frustrated with the special interest. They are frustrated with the special interest because it is hard for them to deal with. It's hard to take away something that is loved by someone so much that it's almost a part of who they are. However, the special interest can cause trouble and be hurtful to the person with autism because they can talk about a subject too much to the point that they overwhelm people. They can lose friendships as a result. As they get older, the special interest or interests can change. Sometimes these can involve other people. For example, it is quite common for an adult with Asperger's Syndrome to develop a special interest in making friends. This is when the interest can become complicated and hard to deal with. Sometimes the interest becomes a fixation with a certain friend leading people to believe the individual with autism is obsessed with the individual. This can be unhealthy to both people. It is also extremely uncomfortable for the person who is the special interest of the individual with autism.

The neurotypical person who wouldn't know much about autism or a special interest would see all of this attention from someone with autism as being borderline obsessive. In this case it is important that we handle the special interest and moderate it as it directly affects other people, but it's also a part of who the person on the autism spectrum really is. So we're in a catch 22 position. We shouldn't change who someone is. But we can't let it affect their interactions with others.

This has been the most frustrating part of my adult life. When making friends, I often heard people say "just be who you are." But then in all reality it's the characteristics of Asperger's Syndrome, such as being clingy or obsessive in social interaction, that scares people away. Those characteristics are a part of who I am. I can't change them or make them go away. But I can learn to control them and modify them as I am doing in my friendship with my best friend now.

Taking the special interest away is not the only solution. A special interest can possibly be modified or toned down with the proper treatment, but it is hard to completely take it away and make it nonexistent. I can totally understand how you could become frustrated with the individual with the interest, so I have thought about effective ways to handle the person's special interest.

First of all, it's extremely crucial that we remember the special interest is not just an interest. The special interest could actually be the person's best friend. So whenever you think about trying to eliminate an interest, please try to remember that you're not really taking away an interest but a friend the person loves. You're also dealing with more than just a want. You're dealing with more of a need. The special interest could be like a need for survival. It could be the only thing that they have to look forward to in life. Taking it away can lead to severe isolation and depression. It's like a leg for a person without autism. Life would be very difficult if you were to lose your legs. If you take a leg away, what happens? You limp around and maybe get by in life, but with the leg you are able to hop, skip, and run just like everyone else.

What I am getting at here is the special interest in an individual with autism can be his or her best friend. So when you're trying to eliminate the special interest in someone with autism, it's going to be painful and uncomfortable to them. Compare it to losing your wife or a close loved one. Obviously, this is going to cause a lot of discomfort. That could be damaging to the individual. So I suggest that as long as the special interest is completely appropriate, we don't try to eliminate it completely. If it's so intense that it's interfering with the person's lifestyle or lifestyles of anyone around the person, then I propose trying to control the intensity level of a special interest. Taking it away from them completely could be tragic.

What if it's an inappropriate interest?

So what do we do if an interest is inappropriate and disturbing to society? I'm not sure there is a good way to handle a situation like this that we know of yet. I had the opportunity to hear about a wonderful young teenager. He has autism and has developed a special interest in girls' feet. Yes a foot fetish. However, because it's a special interest and not just an interest, the intensity level of the interest is overbearing and inappropriate. More often than not you'll find that a special interest is really just a neruotypical person's interest multiplied in intensity, making it a special interest. This teen will walk up to high school girls and tell them that they have beautiful feet. This may come off as a little creepy to the average high school girl. It is situations like this that have been most frustrating in my life.

To an individual with autism, it can be hard to understand the concept of "creepy." Neurotypicals have this filtering system that recognizes when things are a little off or creepy. It's just a feeling that a neurotypical is able to get from their subconscious level. As someone with autism, I don't get this feeling from anyone and am unable to tell or understand when I am putting out this signal to others.

Creepy is frustrating because society has made it out to sound like such a horrible word. When someone says I'm creepy, I automatically feel like I'm a horrible person because I've hurt them in some way. In my mind I think very logically about social situations. To me a lot of social norms and unwritten rules are illogical. I don't understand them. This causes me to make people feel awkward and uncomfortable at times.

One of the things that neurotypicals have an understanding for that I don't is something called "implied meaning." This is a way people communicate with one another without actually saying something. For example, if I call you 25 times today it means something. There's meaning to it. Neurotypicals look for hidden meaning in things and they find it often. Implied meaning is something that I don't understand. How can my actions of me doing something mean something that I haven't verbally told you? I don't get it. But neurotyipcals do.

As I've mentioned, the special interest is like the individuals best friend. So as weird as it might sound, the feet of the girls the teen was interest in are quite possibly like a best friend to him. I have a similar issue with women's arms.

It would be extremely hurtful and tragic to someone with autism if you tried to eliminate the interest in girls' feet entirely. However, there are a couple of options to help diminish how intense it is and how it's affecting those girls who have the beautiful feet.

A special interest can never be eliminated completely. But, it can be controlled. The best way to accomplish this is through Applied Behavioral Analysis, known as ABA therapy in the autism community. The simple definition for ABA therapy is that it's a system of rewards/punishments or take away. When the person complies with a request, they are given positive reinforcement to encourage the chance that they will do it right again and again. The take away is used when the person is unable to comply to a request. Meaning they might not get to play their favorite video game that evening if they didn't meet their goal.

For the guy with the foot interest. We might say "If you can go a day without complimenting girls feet then you can have a reward at the end of the day." If you can't then you won't get to play your favorite video game after school that night.

Another way to approach this would be to try to modify the interest. Notice I said modify, not replace or take away. By modifying it, the person is still able to find enjoyment in the interest but maybe in a different way. Maybe the behavioral consultant could get him to rethink the thought before he says it to a girl.

The consultant should try to get him to not act on his thought so fast. This will allow him time to think and maybe change the thought into something that is more appropriate. If when he has the thought, "Holly has beautiful feet. I'm going to tell her that." We could get him to think and switch to something like, Holly looks really nice today, or Holy is beautiful today, or even, Holly has pretty eyes today, this might come off as a little more appropriate and prevent any tension at school between him and girls. This would make everyone more comfortable with the entire situation.

This is not something that would be easy to do with someone with autism. Trained behavior analyst spend countless hours each week working with children and teens who have autism. It takes an intense approach and a very dedicated therapist to be able to help someone with autism modify behaviors. Applied behavior is in my opinion a gift to the autism community that should be accessed more and covered by more insurance programs.

Importance of Being Able to Escape into Imagination

The ability to escape into imagination is a useful tool for someone who's dealing with Autism or Asperger's Syndrome. I found it to be a way to connect with someone. I used my escape into imagination to connect with actors and actresses in movies. Even though these actors and actresses have no idea who I am, I still feel that I can put on a movie or watch a rerun of Saved by the Bell and connect with these people more than anyone in the world.

It's good for individuals on the spectrum to be able to find this type of connection with someone, even if it is in a make-believe world. Without being able to do this there could be a lot more depression.

Let's face it. Having no one at all to communicate with is lonely. Having someone, whether it be an animal or a make-believe character, to connect with could do wonders for people on the spectrum.

As I get older I am finding that I escape into imagination a little less frequently. Even when I do those make-believe imaginary friends aren't the same as having a real friend. I sometimes create little make believe characters in my mind to be friends with. Seth has been one of them. But, Seth is not like real people. He can't really talk back to me. So it's a one sided conversation.

I think as I get older my I'm able to comprehend more that the make-believe world I create in my mind to help cope with Autism isn't real. When I was younger I believed everything in the make believe world was real. With age, I think I have more capability to recognize the difference between real and fake. It is still difficult and sometimes I do go off on a phase where I live in the make-believe world for a few weeks or a month or so. I have to be snapped out of that phase in order to come back to the real world.

Danger of Escaping Into Imagination

While I do believe that being able to escape into imagination is often extremely beneficial to an individual on the spectrum, I also want to caution of the chance of it becoming a dangerous situation. There's a chance of the person escaping into imagination too often. If this were to happen, the person could seclude themselves from the real world. Even though the real world is often a very hurtful place for us on the spectrum to live in, it is necessary for us to return from that state of imagination and get out into the real world and try to do our best at fitting in and making real friends.

It is important that people with Autism continue to seek out therapy options for improving social skill sets and social thinking. If someone stays in that state of imagination for too long they can become comfortable and believe that state of imagination is their real life. They can stop trying to be a participant in the real world and seclude themselves to their own fantasy world. It's important to have a healthy balance here. The fantasy world that they create can be helpful at times but if it's used or accessed too often can become harmful to themselves and to the friendships and relationships in their life.

I definitely understand how painful and unbearable the real world can be to us at times. People with Autism have likely grown up always being accused of doing something wrong or being annoying. With that said, I can not express how important it is that we continue to try and get out in the real world. Put ourselves out there. Continue to seek out friendships and meet new people. The absolute worst thing we can do is seclude ourselves to a life locked inside of our own homes due to fear of the real world. I often meet people with Autism who are trapped in their own world because they quit trying to be a member of the real world. As hard as it is, we've got to keep trying. Feeling trapped is the worst feeling in the world.

There is irony in this as well. When I am in my make-believe world I often cling to my best friend in real life. Because she's the only tie I have left to the real world at that point and time. Because I've became so socially isolated. Texting her, talking to her, and seeing her are the only ties and connections I have to the real world when I'm at this point and time.

The Autism mind is a very fascinating and complex place to be. While I create a "make believe" world to help me cope with the overwhelming real world, my best friend is my only tie to the real world when I'm in that make believe world. For me, creating the make believe world isn't something that I want to do. I don't necessarily want to be there. But I think it's become a natural response or coping tool for when I feel overwhelmed with something real.

How Can we tell if escaping into imagination is becoming too extreme?

There are a couple of things to watch for here. The main thing is watching to see how the person acts at home. If the individual is still socializing with family members, it's likely okay. However, if it gets to the point where the individual doesn't even want to be around his or her family anymore, there is likely a problem.

The problem being that escaping into imagination or that make-believe world has become too comfortable. There's no pain in there. The individual has no motivation to come back into the real world now because they've managed to find a pain-free and predictable environment.

Tony Attwood says it best in his book The Complete Guide to Asperger's Syndrome. When an individual on the spectrum is by themselves, there is no impairment. The impairment doesn't happen until there is another individual with them. So with the people in their own make-believe world, with no other real human beings around, it becomes safe; life becomes easy, as there is no communication to worry about. I couldn't agree more with what Tony said in his book.

Another way you could catch that this is becoming a problem is if you're able to listen to the individual talk when they're around you. If you feel that they're constantly talking about it like it's becoming their special interest, then it's time to step in and try to modify the make believe world and how it's used.

What is the best way to correct the interest?

There is no clear-cut one size fits all answer. There's not a simple way to bring someone out of their make-believe world and back to the real world. For me, I've had to learn the hard way many times. Many times my make believe world has pushed people away.

This almost happened with my real best friend. Last summer I had this make believe world created where I believed that my best friend was my mother. By continually interacting with her like she was my mother and believing that to be true, I started pushing her away.

I don't think there would have been a good way to come back to reality. I find in most cases with the make believe world for me, I have to be slapped in the face with reality in order to fall out of the make-believe world and find my way back to the real world.

In this case it took my friend being very frustrated after being very patient and understanding saying she couldn't do it anymore. She just couldn't be my mom and couldn't be a part of my make believe world any longer. It was like a wake up call. I knew I had to somehow gain control over my thoughts and come back to reality in order to save the friendship I had with my best friend. It's those real life wake up calls that I think we will find bring people with Autism back into the real world from their own make-believe fantasy world.

Correcting this situation can be very painful for the individual with Autism. Because a make – believe world has become a place of comfort and security, taking that security blanket away will not be easy to do. Please allow time. Giving someone who is on the Autism spectrum time to adjust or time to change something or time do do anything is the best gift that you could ever give them. Often, if the individual is given enough time, they will comply with the request. They just need more time and patience to comply with your request. It takes us longer to process changes.

Giving an Ample Amount of Time for an Individual on the Spectrum to Comply

If you are working with children or young adults on the Autism Spectrum working to correct or modify behaviors, you really need patience. People often expected me to adapt to change or fix something in an instant, without giving me a chance to practice or internalize the thought. This became extremely frustrating for me. I often see people who are so inpatient with each other, but time is something that the individual on the spectrum needs. They need to be able to process your request and then think about it for just a little longer than the average individual who is NT.

I bet if someone were to do a study on people who were on the Autism Spectrum, they would find nearly all, if not all, were able to comply with a request to change a behavior if they were given an ample amount of time.

Physical and Emotional Abuse

For an individual on the Autism spectrum, there can be many things that can present a danger for them. Depending on the severity of the autism, the dangers could range from not being socially aware and making social mistakes or going as far as doing something that's dangerous and could cause them to get hurt or worse. These individuals on the spectrum are just simply not aware of the many dangers of the world. I know for me this has been very much the case through my entire life. I would be easily taken advantage of. Therefore it's crucial that we are aware of this information and can hopefully come up with a way of preventing someone with Autism from being put into harmful, dangerous, uncomfortable situations.

The Friendship/Acquaintance Ratio

It was my junior year. I had no idea about the friendship/acquaintance ratio then. I didn't know what it was or that it even existed. It's actually something I came up with about three or four years ago that I've used as a way of explaining my social interactiosn with people. I often tried extremely hard to develop peer relationships. It seemed like the harder I would try to develop a relationship or friendship with someone the more they would hate me or think I was creepy or psycho. Obviously now I'm aware that they didn't hate me, they were just uncomfortable with me or my behaviors towards them.

The friendship/acquaintance ratio is a relationship between an individual with Autism and a neurotypical. The individual with Autism or Asperger's Syndrome is trying so hard to develop a friendship with the NT that it's an imbalanced equation or ratio.

To the individual on the spectrum, as soon as an NT individual so much as says hi to us and or smiles at us, the NT has become our best friend. While, the NT individual was just saying hi to be friendly and might not even be interested in learning the person on the spectrum's name.

The neurotypical individuals have established a social network that is full of many different people at all different levels of the friendship circle. They have guys that are friends and girls that are friends. Some of them have best friends or acquaintances. Others have co-workers and even more casual friends in that circle as well.

To the neurotypical, meeting the new person won't mean anything at all to them. It will just be "someone they met while they were out and about that night in most cases." Chances are the next day they wouldn't even remember your name or anything about you. Most people have their network of friends established.

The individual with Autism doesn't understand this, and even if he or she did, they still would have a hard time with it because it just makes them feel so good that they didn't get ignored or even worse. The fact that someone actually smiles at me and says hi to me makes me feel good. It never happened much in my past and so when it does I gravitate to it because I really want friends. My reaction is to make that person my best friend right away. The instant they smile or say hi, they can be my best friend.

Because the neurotypical has years of knowing and understanding how to develop friendships appropriately they know that it takes time. They aren't in a rush to bring someone new into their life. I feel a part of this is due to the fact that they themselves have been hurt in friendships and relationships by other neurotypicals.

You see, a common mistake that I made in my younger days with Autism is believing that I was the only one who had trouble making friends or got hurt by other people. I didn't realize that neurotypicals actually can get hurt by other neurotypicals as well. The idea didn't make sense to me. I had this image in my brain that all neurotypicals were amazing and wonderful people that I wanted to be like. As it turns out this simply just isn't the case.

So what happens is that the NT person becomes the person on the spectrum's best friend instantly, while to the NT individual the person on the spectrum just becomes an acquaintance. (Someone they might or might not have an interest in seeing again.)

Due to the excitement in the person on the spectrum, they will become overly anxious and want to develop a friendship with the NT individual more quickly than the NT is comfortable with. This will cause the NT to accuse or assume that the individual on the spectrum is being disrespectful and purposely missing these cues or common knowledge about building a friendship that NT's come preprogrammed with. The person on the spectrum might end up calling the NT too much or too often or texting and e-mailing them too much. They can become overbearing to the NT individual, and they will retreat and try to get rid of the individual on the spectrum.

This is something that has happened to me time and time again. When you end up getting rejected or made fun of, you can't understand because you just don't realize or comprehend what you've done wrong. For me, even when someone would explain it to me, it wouldn't make much sense, and I just couldn't understand why they were reacting that way to me. An example would be with texting. I don't understand how it could be possible to text someone too much. There is nothing harmful about a text message, un less you are saying mean things in it. But if I'm texting someone and I send three hundred nice messages per day, I don't see how this can bother them or upset them. I just don't comprehend it. I feel as if they punish me because I'm nice to them and text them too much in their eyes but I don't understand how or why it's too much. It doesn't register in my brain.

ABOUT THE AUTHOR

I'm Travis. I'm a 27 year old author of books about autism. I like football, basketball, tennis, hiking, music, rock, writing, reading, and talking.

I have overcome the greatest challenge in my life. I no longer cope with autism I live happily with it.

I have some really amazing friends and a truly inspirational and awesome best friend!

Life had always been a struggle for me until I started taking responsibility for my own life and situation. I spent a long time wanting and expecting others to fix or improve my life and make it what I wanted it to be. Truth be known, I was the only one who could and can do that.

Now I write books about autism and how I am taking responsibility for my own life. What a difference I've seen in life.

Life is what we choose to make of it.

I don't want to just be known as a guy with Autism. I want to be known as a guy who's doing something awesome with Autism!

Visit www.travisbreeding.com for more information and other books on Autism. Email Travis at travis@travisbreeding.com

Travis Breeding's Autism Resources

I want to be like you: Life with Asperger's Syndrome

I Want to be Like You
Life with Asperger's Syndrome
by Travis E. Breeding

Something makes Travis Breeding different than everyone else. But it isn't what most people he's met think it is.

Travis Breeding has never been like others. Growing up, he noticed some of the differences—he had a bed-wetting issue; he had difficulty with fine motor skills; he became obsessed with his special interest, trombone; and most troubling for him, he had trouble making friends. He just couldn't seem to fit in with anyone and didn't understand how socializing worked. He couldn't understand why people didn't like him. Why did everyone think he was so weird or creepy or psycho? Was he?

Travis hit a low point in his college days and began making suicide attempts. When he finally learned he has Asperger's, it wasn't quite the solution he longed for. He didn't want to accept it. But once he embraced it, he realized he could begin making changes that could someday lead to living the life he wants—one that includes a family and good friends. And even more, he could help others just like him.

Now Travis is on a mission to help us all understand what Asperger's is and how we can help those around us who seem a little, or a lot, different. With a combination of personal experiences, information about Asperger's and the autism spectrum, and Travis's observations and advice, I Want to be Like You proves to be a perfect tool to help readers who are on the spectrum, are helping someone on the spectrum, or just want to understand what this relatively new diagnosis is to bridge the gap between autistic and neurotypical individuals.

I am a child: Just Like You

I am a child: Just Like You is a story about a little boy named Mason. Mason is unique and special. Follow Mason on his journey exploring the world as he sees it. You will learn that Mason is just like you or any other child. I am a child: Just Like You is aimed to encourage growth of self esteem for children with Autism or other disabilities. It is also a great tool for educating other people about Autism Spectrum Disorders and other Disabilities.

www.travisbreeding.com

https://itunes.apple.com/us/app/i-am-a-child-just-like-you/id495527171?mt=8&ign-mpt=uo%3D4

The Reality of Living Within Two Worlds

What's it like to live and experience Autism? Travis shares his mind and journey with the reader. Come along on his journey and learn about Travis' make believe world that he uses it to cope with Autism. He shares his experiences with the make believe world. He shares how he uses it as a coping mechanism to help get through each day. The make believe world can be a great coping mechanism. It can also be a troubling if too much time is spent inside it. When Travis makes a friend they become like my mother in his mind. The friend is a special interest. He has to try and balance that with the reality of the real world. Travis also explains the relationship between lying and the make believe world of Autism. "This is one of the most moving accounts of growing up with Undiagnosed AS that I have read. Travis Breeding's honesty and willingness to share his struggles with some of the obstacles he faced growing up is a treasure trove for anyone on or off the spectrum. If you have a friend or family member who is different from what you or society expects, this story offers a bird's-eye view of what it might feel like to be in their skin." Maripat Jordan Robison

Autism Social Thinking and Friendship

"Context is King" is a quote by Dr. Peter Gerhardt a Behavior Analyst in the field of Autism. Understanding context is critical for social success. I spent several years trying to master certain social skills. I read books on the subject and even studied with people. It wasn't until I learned about social context that I began to see huge improvements in the area of friendship in my life. People with autism need to learn a social skill set for several different environments. We access a different set of social skills for the club or at a party than we would at the library. We must learn how to access different social channels for various situations. We also need to understand the different context of each social relationship. A good friendship is not the same context as a co-worker. We must learn how to behave differently with the co-worker than we do our friend. This book will help your child or student learn the different channels or contexts of social relationships.

Made in United States
North Haven, CT
26 November 2021